IT'S OK TO FAIL IT'S OK TO FAIL

This journal belongs to

_____,

(not) a failure.

Created, published, and distributed by Knock Knock
6080 Center Drive
Los Angeles, CA 90045
knockknockstuff.com
Knock Knock is a registered trademark of
Knock Knock LLC

© 2019 Knock Knock LLC
All rights reserved
Printed in China

No part of this product may be used or reproduced in any manner whatsoever without prior written permission from the publisher, except in the case of brief quotations embodied in critical articles and reviews. For information, address Knock Knock.

Where specific company, product, and brand names are cited, copyright and trademarks associated with these names are property of their respective owners. Every reasonable attempt has been made to identify owners of copyright. Errors or omissions will be corrected in subsequent editions.

ISBN: 978-168349188-0
UPC: 825703-50190-2

10 9 8 7 6 5 4 3 2 1

IT'S OK
TO FAIL

Today's Note-to-Self: It's OK to fail at…

Failure is authentic, and because
and because of that, it's a pure

it's authentic, it's real and genuine,
state of being. Douglas Coupland

Today's Note-to-Self: It's OK to be totally…

To do any kind of creative work well, you have to run at stuff knowing that it's usually going to fail…In my experience, most stuff that you start is mediocre for a really long time before it actually gets good.

Ira Glass

Today's Note-to-Self: It's OK to wish that…

When I first started telling people that I wanted to be a writer... people would say, "Aren't you afraid you're never going to have any success? Aren't you afraid the humiliation of rejection will kill you? Aren't you afraid that you're going to work your whole life at this craft and nothing's ever going to come of it and you're going to die on a scrap heap of broken dreams with your mouth filled with bitter ash of failure?" The short answer to all those questions is yes. Yes, I am afraid of all those things and I always have been, and I am afraid of many many more things besides that people can't even guess at—like seaweed, and other things that are scary.

Elizabeth Gilbert

We are all stinking messes, every last one of us, or we once were messes and found our way out, or we are trying to find our way out of a mess, scratching, reaching.

Roxane Gay

Today's Note-to-Self: It's OK if people think I'm…

Today's Note-to-Self: It's OK to do things like…

I fell off my pink cloud

with a thud. Elizabeth Taylor

Welcome to
the real world!
It sucks! You're
gonna love it.

Monica, *Friends*

Today's Note-to-Self: It's OK to be super excited about…

Today's Note-to-Self: It's OK to not…

Success is a lousy teacher. It seduces smart

people into thinking they can't lose. Bill Gates

People who say nothing inspires them more than "no" and how rejection fuels them WHAT IS THAT LIKE? Also are you lying?

Mary H. K. Choi

Today's Note-to-Self: It's OK to speak up about…

Today's Note-to-Self: It's OK that my bestie and I…

Be anything you like, be madmen, drunks, and bastards of every shape and form, but at all costs avoid one thing: success… If you are too obsessed with success, you will forget to live. If you have learned only how to be a success, your life has probably been wasted.

Thomas Merton

Today's Note-to-Self: It's OK to treat myself to…

Write down everything you fear in life. Burn it. Pour herbal oil with a sweet scent on the ashes.

Yoko Ono

Today's Note-to-Self: It's OK if I start…

Whenever a friend succeeds, a

little something in me dies. Gore Vidal

Today's Note-to-Self: It's OK to lose…

I don't mind failing in this world,
I don't mind failing in this world,
Somebody else's definition
Doesn't measure my soul's condition,
I don't mind failing in this world.

Malvina Reynolds

If everyone had always laughed at my jokes, I wouldn't have figured out how to be so funny. If they hadn't told me I was ugly, I never would have searched for my beauty. And if they hadn't tried to break me down, I wouldn't know that I'm unbreakable.

Gabourey Sidibe

Today's Note-to-Self: It's OK to be hurt when…

Today's Note-to-Self: It's OK to be, like,…

> Most people, after one success, are so cringingly afraid of doing less well that they rub all the edge off their subsequent work.
>
> Beatrix Potter

Today's Note-to-Self: It's OK to go all out and…

What makes people resilient and irony in situations that would

is the ability to find humor
otherwise overpower you.   Amy Tan

I've etched out who I am through myriad haircut attempts, outfit attempts, beauty attempts, diet attempts. It's been an evolution.

Jamie Lee Curtis

Today's Note-to-Self: It's OK to need more…

Today's Note-to-Self: It's OK that I'm so…

Nobody tells you about failure…People always talk about winning, vision boards, getting what you want. People also don't talk about fear. It's always keeping fear at bay. Squelching it. Throwing it away. I've embraced fear and failure as a part of my success. I understand that it's part of the grand continuum of life. I've been through it all.

Viola Davis

Today's Note-to-Self: It's OK to high-five myself for…

Remember that not getting
a wonderful stroke

what you want is sometimes
of luck. The Dalai Lama

Today's Note-to-Self: It's OK to believe…

Only a man who knows what it is like to be defeated can reach down to the bottom of his soul and come up with the extra ounce of power it takes to win when the match is even.

Muhammad Ali

My wisdom to share, I think, is really about not giving up—ever. And I think that's a really important thing, that I just keep going.
And all of these minor failures don't phase me. I really just enjoy every day, and I think we just have to. You just can't give up, no matter what.

Margaret Cho

Today's Note-to-Self: It's OK for me and you-know-who to…

Today's Note-to-Self: It's OK if it takes me…

Keep away from people who try to belittle
but the really great make you feel that

your ambition. Small people always do that,
you, too, can become great.   Mark Twain

Today's Note-to-Self: It's OK to feel all the feels when…

You build on failure. You use it as a stepping stone. Close the door on the past. You don't try to forget the mistakes, but you don't dwell on it. You don't let it have any of your energy, or any of your time, or any of your space.

Johnny Cash

Today's Note-to-Self: It's OK to vent by…

When we lose one blessing, another is often

most unexpectedly given in its place.   C. S. Lewis

We are so lucky to be alive, whether we're 35 or 55 or 105, and it's never too late to make a small, safe space for yourself, where you can say, without fear, "I have more to give. I am going to try and fail. It's okay to try. Failing is good for you." Trying is brave. Failing is brave. FLAILING IS FREEDOM. Embrace glitches and discouragement and entropy. Prepare to feel ashamed. Sometimes you feel the most shame at the exact moment when you're reaching out for your truest source of happiness.

Heather Havrilesky

Today's Note-to-Self: It's OK to secretly hope…

I've had all my big successes on the heels of rejection and frankly, it's right up my alley… I consider your rejection a lucky charm.

Barbara Corcoran

Today's Note-to-Self: It's OK that I don't always…

Today's Note-to-Self: It's OK to want…

Time is a strange thing. I was at rock bottom and out of money, with no work in sight, but one step at a time, it gets better. It gets much better than better.

Ellen DeGeneres

Today's Note-to-Self: It's OK when…

I missed more than 9,000 shots in my career.
I have been trusted to take the game-winning
over and over again in my life. And

I've lost almost 300 games. Twenty-six times shot… and missed. I have failed over and that is why I succeed.   Michael Jordan

Today's Note-to-Self: It's OK to be confused about…

"There is no point at which you can say, 'Well, I'm successful now. I might as well take a nap.'"

Carrie Fisher

Whether you succeed or not is irrelevant, there is no such thing. Making your unknown known is the important thing—and keeping the unknown always beyond you.

Georgia O'Keeffe

Today's Note-to-Self: It's OK to be seriously…

Today's Note-to-Self: It's OK to say…

You tried your best and
The lesson is "never try."

you failed miserably.
Homer Simpson, *The Simpsons*

Today's Note-to-Self: It's OK to LOL about…

One of the things I learned the hard way was that it doesn't pay to get discouraged. Keeping busy and making optimism a way of life can restore your faith in yourself.

Lucille Ball

What if you do fail, and get fairly rolled in the dirt once or twice? Up again, you shall never more be so afraid of a tumble.

Ralph Waldo Emerson

Today's Note-to-Self: It's OK to feel iffy about…

Today's Note-to-Self: It's OK that it drives me bonkers when…

To the young artist who may be reading this:
actually be lucky when you get rejected
appeared to be bad luck, I fell into

consider the possibility that you might
from stuff. Because of this streak of what
my life as it is today. Lisa Yuskavage

Attitude, it's all an attitude. Just because you fail, don't mean you have to lose.

Dolly Parton

Today's Note-to-Self: It's OK to wonder…

Today's Note-to-Self: It's OK if I stop…

Shake it off.

Taylor Swift

Today's Note-to-Self: It's OK to show…

> One could wait a lifetime, and find nothing at the end of the waiting. I would begin here, I would make something happen.
>
> Louis L'Amour

Failure meant a stripping away of the inessential. I stopped pretending to myself that I was anything other than what I was and began to direct all my energy into finishing the only work that mattered to me... And so rock bottom became the solid foundation on which I rebuilt my life.

J. K. Rowling

Today's Note-to-Self: It's OK that I didn't…

The reality is: sometimes you lose. And you're never too good to lose. You're never too big to lose. You're never too smart to lose. It happens.

Beyoncé Knowles

Today's Note-to-Self: It's OK that I'm not...

Today's Note-to-Self: It's OK to think it's cool when…

In any case you mustn't confuse a single

failure with a final defeat. F. Scott Fitzgerald

Today's Note-to-Self: It's OK because…

The important thing is this: to be able at any moment to sacrifice what we are for what we could become.

Charles Du Bos

What I tell these young people is, the world is not as dangerous as the older generation would like you to believe. Anyone I know who has ever taken a risk and lost a job has ended up getting a better one two years later.

Jonathan Kozol

Today's Note-to-Self: It's OK to spend…

Sometimes people let the same problem make them miserable for years when they could just say, "So what." That's one of my favorite things to say. "So what."

Andy Warhol

Today's Note-to-Self: It's OK to have a…

Today's Note-to-Self: It's OK to wanna cry about…

Do you like to draw with crayons? I'm not very good at it. But it doesn't matter. It's the fun of doing it that's important… In a way, you've already won in this world because you're the only one who can be you.

Mr. Rogers

Today's Note-to-Self: It's OK to wear…

In spite of everything I shall rise again: I will my great discouragement, and I will go

take up my pencil, which I have forsaken in
on with my drawing. Vincent Van Gogh

Sometimes life hits you in the head with a brick. Don't lose faith.

Steve Jobs

Today's Note-to-Self: It's OK that I kind of blew it when…

Today's Note-to-Self: It's OK blah blah blah…

I don't like people who have never fallen and of little value. Life hasn't revealed

or stumbled. Their virtue is lifeless
its beauty to them.   Boris Pasternak

Today's Note-to-Self: It's OK to rant about…

Making your mark on the world is hard. If it were easy, everybody would do it. But it's not. It takes patience, it takes commitment, and it comes with plenty of failure along the way.

Barack Obama

Today's Note-to-Self: It's OK if people don't…

> I didn't lose the gold. I won the silver.
>
> Michelle Kwan

I learned, especially in school, to value "success" and to hide "failure" so that I wouldn't be scolded or ridiculed. That wasn't the way that I had started out, when *both* were interesting, and failure was sometimes more stimulating than success because it raised more questions.

Barry Stevens

Today's Note-to-Self: It's OK to love…

Today's Note-to-Self: It's OK to hate it when…

Turn your wounds into wisdom. You will
You'll make mistakes. Some people will call them
God's way of saying, "Excuse me, you're

be wounded many times in your life.
failures, but I have learned that failure is really
moving in the wrong direction."   Oprah Winfrey

There is much to be said for failure. It is more interesting than success.

Max Beerbohm

Today's Note-to-Self: It's OK to say screw it and…

There is nothing in the world so easy to explain as failure—it is, after all, what everybody does all the time.

Susanna Clarke

Today's Note-to-Self: It's OK to need less…

Today's Note-to-Self: It's OK that I haven't got…

I don't believe in regrets. I
every hardship I've gone through
testimony if you've

believe every mistake I've made,
gives me testimony. You cannot have
not been tested.   Laverne Cox

Today's Note-to-Self: It's OK that I still…

The worst tragedy that could have befallen me was my success.

Jonas Salk

Today's Note-to-Self: It's OK to freak out because…

> Life is to be lived, not controlled; and humanity is won by continuing to play in the face of certain defeat.
>
> Ralph Ellison

Today's Note-to-Self: It's OK even if…

Flops are a part of life's
miss out on any of the

menu and I'm never a girl to courses. Rosalind Russell

If at first you don't succeed, failure may be your style.

Quentin Crisp

Today's Note-to-Self: It's OK to ask for…

You have been criticizing yourself for years, and it hasn't worked. Try approving of yourself and see what happens.

Louise L. Hay

Today's Note-to-Self: It's OK to hold on to…

Today's Note-to-Self: It's OK that I couldn't even…

We are all failures—at least

all the best of us are.   J. M. Barrie

Today's Note-to-Self: It's OK when I miss…

I'm good at losing. It's one of my specialties.

Anthony Kiedis

I was never interested in the bit where [fairy tale heroines] became amazing, and everyone was like, "you're so amazing." It was the falling and getting up, and the falling and getting up, and what changed between each fall and each rise…that was the real story for me.

Helen Oyeyemi

Today's Note-to-Self: It's OK to create…

Today's Note-to-Self: It's OK to be pissed about…

I look at rejections as a badge
first hundred, you're not even

of honor. Until you have your a real writer. Janet Fitch

Today's Note-to-Self: It's OK to feel…

To be an artist is to fail, as no other dare fail.

Samuel Beckett

Today's Note-to-Self: It's OK to like it when…

Don't buy society's definition of success. Because it's not working for anyone. It's not working for women, it's not working for men, it's not working for polar bears, it's not working for the cicadas that are apparently about to emerge and swarm us. It's only truly working for those who make pharmaceuticals for stress, diabetes, heart disease, sleeplessness, and high blood pressure.

Arianna Huffington

Today's Note-to-Self: It's OK to think that…

Winning is great, sure, but if you are really learning how to lose. Nobody goes undefeated all and go on to win again, you are going to

going to do something in life, the secret is
the time. If you can pick up after a crushing defeat,
be a champion someday.   Wilma Rudolph

> Success is really defined by how quickly you dust yourself and be like, "Girl, I still love you, get the next one."
>
> — Jonathan Van Ness

Today's Note-to-Self: It's OK to give myself a break because…

I function better when things are going badly than when they're as smooth as whipped cream. When I'm in a fight I don't worry, but when things are going good I'm afraid that something's going to crack under me any minute. You may not realize it when it happens, but a kick in the teeth may be the best thing in the world for you.

Walt Disney

Today's Note-to-Self: It's OK to spend too much time…

Today's Note-to-Self: It's OK to get mad when…

Have you ever noticed how "What the hell" is always the right decision to make?

Terry Johnson

Today's Note-to-Self: It's OK to let go of…

Sometimes I feel like my whole life has

been one big rejection. Marilyn Monroe

Today's Note-to-Self: It's OK that I…

I discovered that rejections are not altogether a bad thing. They teach a writer to rely on his own judgment and to say in his heart of hearts, "To hell with you."

Saul Bellow

Go forth and fall,
flail, and fly.